S. ANSELM'S LI[BRARY]

CW01574599

Superstars Omnibus II

04198

The Superstars Series

Superstars Omnibus II

Chris Hudson

RMEP

RELIGIOUS AND MORAL EDUCATION PRESS

Contents

The Scale Model

The ship's hold stank. Oh no … he was going to be sick! Thomas quickly scrambled back up the ladder to get a few breaths of fresh air.

'Sorry about that!' the ship's doctor whispered from underneath. He was below deck at the foot of the ladder, staring up and looking worried. 'I forgot to warn you about the stink. We get used to it, you see. Quick! Get back down here before someone notices you!'

Thomas held his breath, then climbed back down the ladder into the hold, dreading the moment when he would have to open his lungs again and take in the awful stench. He tried it, coughed, then gradually started breathing normally, trying to think of anything else that would stop him from feeling sick – but it was difficult. The air was thick with a foul odour.

'Do you think *this* is bad?' muttered the ship's doctor. 'You should smell it when it's *full*!'

'Tell me about it,' replied Thomas, taking out his notebook and pencil, 'I want to know everything.' As the doctor began to speak, Thomas started to write furiously.

'Well, in this hold they fit in about four hundred and fifty bodies. You look surprised? Sometimes they can fit in two or three times that number! They put them in lying down, allowing each one a space of about four foot by one foot. Sometimes it's less. Remember that they have to be chained as well, to stop them running about! They stay in that position for the whole voyage, except when we bring them up on deck to have a little exercise and fresh air.'

'What about fresh water and food?'

'That gets lowered down in buckets for them, and the food is often just a cold vegetable stew. It's not enough, I keep telling the captain that, but he says that he can afford to lose a few of the weak ones because he can sell the fit ones at such an amazing profit. He says that they're just creatures, after all, and they don't feel pain the way we do. Sometimes, we've lost half of them through disease. The bodies just get thrown overboard.' He paused, picturing it, then added. 'We see a lot of sharks following us sometimes.'

Thomas turned angrily on him. 'What do *you* think? You're the ship's *doctor*! You should know if a living creature can feel pain.'

The other man paused, then spoke. 'Yes, I think they *do* feel pain. At night, we can hear all sorts of awful noises coming up from the hold, especially when we're going through bad weather. Most of the crew say they've felt uneasy about it at times, but for them it's just a job. They're only following orders. They all have families to support in Bristol. Somebody has to pay their wages, and for many of them, it's either this or join the Navy, and only an idiot does that. "A man's got to live." That's what they always say – a man's got to live.'

'Do *you* say that?' Thomas stared hard at the doctor, who looked away, embarrassed. Thomas felt angry with him, then sorry for being so rude – the man was helping him after all, and he could lose his job just for showing Thomas around the ship. But what was that he said? 'A man's got to live?' Thomas gazed around the hold, his eyes now used to the darkness.

You wouldn't keep cattle in these conditions! So why were they treating people like this? Innocent men, women and children were being captured, bought and sold like cattle, chained up and dragged away from their native lands in Africa, to be forced to

The triangular trade

The African (or Bristol) Trade worked in a triangular pattern, with some ships working all three of the routes. Slaves were taken from Africa to America, and cash crops were taken from America to Britain and the rest of Europe. Goods were then produced in Britain and Europe to sell or exchange for slaves in Africa. Neat, wasn't it? Slavery made a great deal of business for so many people …

work as slaves in the sugar plantations of Jamaica. Thousands died during the crossing. Families were torn apart, husbands separated from their wives and parents torn away from their children. It was all incredibly cruel, but no one in England seemed to care – after all, it made the country rich and produced the sugar that everyone liked to stir into their tea. But it had to stop! The whole awful business had to stop!

Slavery now

Slavery still exists today! You can find out more from Anti-Slavery International on **www.antislavery.org/** and from the Anti-Slavery Society on **www.antislaverysociety.addr.com/** and **www.childlabor.net/**

Thomas felt helpless. What would it take to convince people that the slave trade was barbaric? How could he convince people that the whole filthy business was *wrong*? Nobody would believe him. He stared around the ship's hold again in disgust. How many people had died forgotten in this floating dungeon? How many tears had been shed? This was an evil place, but few really knew about it, and those who did, didn't seem to care. How could he make decent people sit up and listen and *care*?

Then all of a sudden, he had an idea. He picked up the notepad and started drawing. He took some rough measurements, pacing up and down and then jotting down the numbers on a diagram that quickly took shape. If only he'd brought a measuring stick! Oh well, this would do for now. The ship's doctor was curious at this change in behaviour.

'What are you doing? I thought you only wanted to write down everything I said.'

'I'm making some sketches.'

'What for?'

'You'll see.'

'No one shall be held in slavery or servitude; slavery and the slave trade shall be prohibited in all their forms'

Article 4, Universal Declaration of Human Rights

Later that day, Thomas set to work in his study. He took out some large sheets of paper and started making sketches of the inside of the ship. Let's see … he'd have to think about getting the exact sizes right, so he'd need help from someone who understood ships and scale, and he might have to make another visit, to check that the measurements were as exact as possible.

How big was the whole ship again? How many slaves did it carry? All the details would have to be exactly right.

A few weeks later, Thomas invited the ship's doctor round to his house. 'I've got something to show you!' he said grinning proudly, holding something up to the light.

'A model ship?' asked the doctor, taking it in his hands and looking a little puzzled. 'That's something the old sailors make for a hobby! It's a bit big. What's all this about? I thought you had your mind on higher things!'

'I have. Look closer!'

Taking the model back, Thomas set it down on the table, fiddled with some catches and took the main hull of the ship apart, in layers. The doctor studied the model closely.

'Oh … *now* I see.' He gave a low whistle.

It was a scale model of the slave ship, designed to open out into parts that showed each of the decks in detail. Hundreds of slaves were shown lying down in the hold, chained to the floor, packed together like peas in a pod, with no space to move – just as they were in real life. If you could have taken a real slave ship apart, then this is what it would have looked like. The doctor was impressed.

'What are you going to do with it?'

'I'm going to send it to a friend. Have you heard of William Wilberforce?' The doctor nodded. 'He's planning a campaign with me. We're going to put a stop to this buying and selling of human lives. This model will show people the truth about what a slave ship is really like inside. It might take years, but we'll do it, because it's right and God is with us. It'll be a long fight, but in the end, we'll win. We'll do it by persuading people, telling them what's going on, showing them the truth about the slave trade – and as our Lord said, the Truth will set people free, all over again.'

He held part of the model up to the light, and looked closely at the little bodies huddled up together on one of the decks.

'Yes,' he muttered. 'One day, they'll see.'

The scale model

This scale model was created to convey the sheer awfulness of conditions on a slaver ship. It still remains a powerful image. Remember – the slave trade was all about making money. Each slave arriving safely in the Americas could be worth thousands of pounds in today's money.

A time-line for slavery

1444	Portugal first imports slaves from Africa.
1496	Christopher Columbus brings back 'Indian' slaves to Portugal from America.
1510	King Ferdinand of Spain approves sale of African slaves in America.
1672	King Charles II of England approves setting up of Royal African Company for slave trade.
1772	Slavery abolished within England. (No *English person* allowed to be a slave.)
1778	Slavery abolished within Scotland. (No *Scottish person* allowed to be a slave.)
1780	By this time, about 70 000 African slaves were being taken across the Atlantic to America *every year*.
1783	Clarkson and Wilberforce's 'Committee for Effecting the Abolition of the Slave Trade' formed.
1807	Slave trade abolished by Britain and its colonies.
1833	Slavery itself abolished in British colonies.
1839	'British and Foreign Anti-Slavery Society' formed, aiming to abolish slavery throughout the world (now called 'Anti-Slavery International').

The long struggle

Thomas Clarkson was born in 1760, did well at school, and went to college in Cambridge. He was a rising star: in 1785 he wrote a prize-winning essay entitled 'Is it lawful to make men slaves against their will?' Then his life changed, on a journey to London. He was trying to find a publisher when he says he 'had a vision'. God had told him to devote the rest of his life to abolishing the slave trade. Clarkson went on to London and found a publisher. Meanwhile, a 'Committee for Effecting the Abolition of the Slave Trade' was being formed, including such names as William Wilberforce MP, John Wesley (the Methodist preacher) and Josiah Wedgwood (of pottery fame). Clarkson joined them and became the campaign researcher.

He journeyed to slaving ports such as Liverpool and Bristol, carried out hundreds of interviews and produced masses of evidence. The campaign took a long time. The Slavery Abolition Act wasn't passed until 1833, but it gave all slaves within the British Empire a new level of freedom. Clarkson retired to Ipswich, where he died in 1846. Without him, British slavery would have continued for much longer. His success also turned the British Navy into a powerful force for good – its West Africa Squadron began to hunt down slave ships and set their prisoners free. Slavery still continued in the USA until the end of the American Civil War in 1865, and in Brazil until the 1890s. *It still exists now*. To find out more, see 'Slavery now' on page 6.

Slavery in history

'Slave: a person who is the legal property of another or others, and is bound to absolute obedience.'
(Oxford Encyclopedic Dictionary)

Slavery has existed for thousands of years in many different forms. In biblical times, it was an organised way of keeping servants, but slaves could always choose to leave a master after a number of years. In Roman times, you could (if you were lucky) pay your way out of slavery to become a freedman. (Most of the gladiators who fought in the Roman arena were slaves or captured prisoners.)

Fighting back

Many black slaves played their own part in the battle against slavery. There were numerous slave revolts on land and sea, some of the most successful being on the island of Haiti, and on the ship *Amistad* (a story now filmed by Steven Spielberg). Also, many free black people helped to smuggle escaped slaves to freedom. Harriet Tubman later became famous for organising a whole network called the 'Underground Railroad' in the USA, with secret passwords and 'safe houses'. Some escaped slaves (including Oladah Equiano and Frederick Douglas) also published their own stories as part of the public campaign.

Making money

In the seventeenth century, slavery was seen as the only possible way to provide workers to grow cash crops like sugar, cotton and tobacco on the farms and plantations of America – and the best place to find workers who could cope with the climate was in Africa. Villages would be raided, prisoners would be taken, then marched to the coast. There they were sold on to traders who took them away by ship and sold them to landowners in America. Many Africans made a lot of money from this, as each captive was worth hundreds or thousands of pounds in modern money.

Some people (and ports like Liverpool and Bristol) also grew incredibly rich. They fought hard to keep it that way, just as modern dealers do to protect their trade in illegal drugs. About 10–13 million people were taken from Africa during that time period, never to return. We still don't know exactly how many suffered like this, and never will. Each one of those millions of people was a person just like you and me.

Missionaries

Some of the unsung heroes and heroines of this time were the missionaries who went out to teach the slaves about Christianity, and who also sent back secret information from the plantations to Clarkson. (Many are still remembered with great affection in the Caribbean.) They were blamed for 'giving the slaves ideas' and organising slave revolts. Slave owners did not like the idea of slaves becoming Christians, because it meant that the slaves were human beings just like themselves. Some missionaries even sold *themselves* into slavery, so that slaves could hear about Jesus! Christianity is sometimes seen as the religion of the oppressors. But here, it wasn't!

The Final Treatment

Elder Long was so pleased! It was a sunny day, perfect for everything that he had been planning. The football stadium was filling up, and there were lots of policemen watching the crowd. Long gave a nod to the director of music, and the band began to play cheerfully. Soon, the Dancers of the Revolution would come out to perform for the crowd as the band played, weaving their ribbons and flags in a swirl of exciting colourful patterns. Long had spent a great deal of money on these dancers and musicians. It was all worth it, now. It *had* to be.

He gazed around the impressive stadium and smiled. Yes, this was what it was all about. There were red flags everywhere, with yards and yards of bunting flapping in the stiff breeze. He felt proud to be Chinese, and proud to be part of the Revolution in Yunnan province. Today would be remembered as *his* day. The Party leaders always said that the Party would reward 'acts of outstanding service'. Today would convince them.

Long sat back in his chair. He could almost relax now, because it was all going to plan. The crowd

China – the sleeping giant?

The people of China were ruled by powerful emperors and warlords for thousands of years. The Chinese invented many new products such as gunpowder and paper, but some of their leaders were suspicious of 'change'. By the 1800s, they were being outclassed by other modern countries that could create things like medicine, steamboats or rifles. China was thought to be a very 'backward' place: attractive to look at, but behind the times. In the Victorian era, some Western traders in China actually started and encouraged a massive trade in opium (a powerful drug), creating thousands of Chinese addicts! They were even supported by the British Navy, who fought the Chinese government when they tried to stop it! Things like that aren't forgotten quickly.

How China changed in 1949

During the Second World War against Japan, many Chinese decided it was time to rebuild their country from scratch. This led to a revolution in 1949 and a new government for 'The People's Republic of China'. Their new message could be summed up as: 'If it's not Chinese, it's bad.' Foreigners were sent home, and anything 'foreign' was attacked, including religions introduced by foreigners such as Christianity, Islam and Buddhism. These attacks grew worse in the 1960s, during the time called the 'Cultural Revolution'. A lot of people ended up dead or in prison as the Chinese government and its student supporters (the Red Guards) tore their country apart, looking for enemies to blame their problems on! That's where Elder Long got started ...

were clapping along with the music and enjoying the dancers, who were now performing on a big stage at the centre of the football pitch. This was the way ahead, he thought – with music and dance and colour. Give the people this, and they won't need *anything* else. They won't need religion any more.

He had come a long way himself. He remembered all the time he'd been at religious college, training as a Christian minister. It now looked so stupid, but it had been useful, because it showed him how the enemy worked. These Christians fooled people with all their talk of a loving God who cared. Huh! It was just a smoke-screen to keep the poor from seeing the truth and asking awkward questions! China was different now. The Revolution was sweeping away all these lies.

He'd realised that on a tour of Beijing, on a summer's day in 1951. He was taken to see the Imperial Temple of Heaven and shown the famous Echo Wall. The Emperors had used the Wall to make their voices sound like those of the gods when they spoke to the people – but it was just a clever trick using sound waves and a smooth surface that made a human voice sound weird. He'd even tried it out for himself. 'LISTEN TO MY VOICE, I SOUND LIKE A GOD!' he'd said in a deep voice, with the echo bouncing around the hall. That's how people get fooled, he thought. That's how religion works – it's all a trick! He decided he wasn't a fool, and left the college. Now he was a keen supporter of the local Communist Party in Sapushan district.

He knew the truth now. People didn't need God. It was as simple as that. If they wanted to put some colour into their drab lives, they went to church. But now, he would give them something better. He would provide concerts of music, theatre and dance. The people just needed a bit of 'culture', not religion.

Of course, it hadn't been as simple as that. Superstition is like an infectious disease or a cancer – sometimes it has to be cut out. He knew that now. Elder Long felt he was like a surgeon holding a sharp scalpel, cutting out all the crazy ideas that kept people stupid. Every time he burned a Bible or put another church leader in prison, he knew he was doing more good, and making China more fit and healthy. Today would be the *final* treatment.

The 'surgeon'

Elder Long was a church member until the 1960s, when he joined the 'Red Guards' – the student groups who supported the 'Cultural Revolution'. The police often just stood by and let them get on with wrecking someone's house or burning all the 'wrong' books in a library. People like Elder Long were allowed to do whatever they wanted. He was put in charge of the 'irreligious model' experiment, to see if people could be steered away from religion by providing other things for them to do, like going to the theatre. It didn't work. He was still furious about this when someone interviewed him about it in 1988! (What's more, he didn't think the government was grateful enough for all the good things he had done!)

They had rounded up all the Christians in Sapushan district and brought them to the stadium. They had a leader called Wang Zhiming, but he had already been arrested, put on trial, then sentenced to death for being an enemy of the Revolution. Elder Long had been there when the sentence was read out in court. What a victory! The Red Guards had cheered and clapped. But it wouldn't be enough to execute Wang Zhiming in prison where no one would see it. Something like this would have to be done in public, in front of all the people that Wang Zhiming had fooled with his stupid lies about a God who cared. Then they would *see* what happens to liars. If you cut off the disease at its root, then the disease would die.

Persecution: subjecting a person to hostility or ill-treatment, especially on political or religious grounds.

The chief of police came over to where Long was sitting. 'The crowd are getting restless, sir. I think you'd better do something.'

Elder Long frowned. The programme of music and dance was only halfway through, but never mind. 'Very well. Bring out the prisoner.' He barked out some orders, and the Dancers of the Revolution were sent back to their places, looking slightly confused. Then with a roll of drums, the band started to play some new music, the Chinese national anthem. Everybody rose, standing to attention – and then the prisoner was brought out.

'It's Wang!' he heard someone shout. A few people started to applaud, but the policemen stopped them. The prisoner was brought out to stand on the platform, facing the place where Elder Long and his officials were sitting. Wang Zhiming was surrounded by a lot of guards, but he didn't look particularly dangerous. In fact, he looked rather frail. That's the way it is with liars, thought Long. You can't see how dangerous they really are. He rose and stepped up towards his microphone.

'Wang Zhiming,' he shouted, 'you have been arrested, tried in the people's court, and found guilty of being an enemy of the Chinese people! Your lies have twisted the minds of hundreds of good, decent folk, and you have been sentenced to death. Is there anything you wish to say to the people before the sentence is carried out?'

The old man nodded and stepped forward away from his guards towards a nearby microphone. Elder Long smiled. This whole speech had already been agreed with Wang, who had asked that his family's lives be spared if he could just say three things to the crowd. Long listened, then agreed. He couldn't see anything dangerous in Wang's final message, once he'd heard it. Let him speak.

Wang coughed, then spoke clearly into the microphone.

'I will tell the people what I have said to my own family. Firstly, you should not follow my example. Secondly, you should follow the words from above and repent once again. Thirdly, in all of your work, you should pay attention to cleanliness.'

Some of the crowd started applauding when they heard this, which sounded odd to Elder Long. Hadn't Wang been confessing to spreading all those lies about God?

The police chief turned to Long. 'Did you agree that little speech with him?' He nodded, but the police chief frowned. 'I just hope we don't regret it!'

'Why?'

'Look at them!' He pointed over at the crowd on the other side of the stadium. Some of them were actually waving at Wang Zhiming as he was taken down to the place of execution. 'You and I know what we heard, but I think it meant something else to that lot over there!'

Elder Long wasn't sure. 'Let's get on with the sentence,' he ordered. Wang was made to kneel by the executioner. He held his hands together in prayer, said something to the executioner, then bowed his head. The blow fell. Wang's body collapsed to the ground and lay still. At another signal from Long, it was dragged away by the guards.

'And so it ends,' muttered Long, signalling to the band, who started playing a cheerful march tune. But something was wrong – the crowd weren't sitting down. He could hear some of them shouting. Others were waving their fists. He was just sitting back in his seat when he saw some women shoving past the guards and making their way across the pitch to where he sat. What was going on? The women weren't armed, but they looked furious.

'That was disgusting!' shouted one of them, pointing up at him.

'And you call yourself a leader of the people? A murderer, more like!' added another.

'Wang Zhiming never hurt a soul! He wasn't guilty of anything!' shouted another. 'You can keep your Revolution if it kills a good man like him!'

The police moved forward to arrest them, but stopped and looked around. More of the crowd were leaving their places and striding out on to the pitch. They were heading this way, and they outnumbered the police. Some were holding bits of wood that they'd torn down. Flags were being ripped up.

'Stop them!' shouted Long to the chief of police.

'It's too late for that!' he replied. 'You'd better leave now *while you still can*!'

He grabbed Long and hustled him through a door, down some steps and out of the stadium into a waiting car. It was nearly too late. Some of the crowd were pushing their way through the line of police to get at him, and even trying to throw a few punches! Long was bundled into the car by the chief of police – and with a screech of tyres, they were quickly driven away.

What had gone

The secret message

What was Wang Zhiming talking about in his final message? People in Yunnan still talk about it. Most of them say he meant this:

'Firstly, you should not follow my example.'
(Follow Jesus' example instead!)

'Secondly, you should follow the words from above and repent once again.'
(Do what God says, not these so-called people in authority!)

'Thirdly, in all of your work, you should pay attention to cleanliness.'
(Be good in every possible way!)

A dangerous enemy

Wang Zhiming had been a Christian since childhood, employed first as a school teacher and then as a church minister. The authorities considered him to be a 'model worker', until the 'Cultural Revolution' came in the 1960s. (See 'How China changed in 1949'.) Wang criticised the way that the authorities encouraged people to confess their own 'crimes' and produce names of other local 'enemies of the people'. He refused to 'name names', was listed as an 'enemy of the people', and finally arrested in 1969. He was murdered in front of a mass rally of 10 000 people in 1973, where this story takes place.

wrong? Long rubbed at the bruise on the back of his head as the car sped along the road. He couldn't understand it.

'We need to spend more money!' he muttered. 'We've got to show these people how foolish they are!'

The police chief turned round in his seat and glared. 'Excuse me, sir, but did you say your wanted to spend *more* money? Would you please tell me *who's* been paying those people to be Christians?' Long fell silent, because he knew the answer – *nobody*. It didn't make any sense at all. Some people just didn't know who their friends really were!

Blessed are you when people insult you, persecute you and falsely say all kinds of evil against you because of me. Rejoice and be glad, because great is your reward in heaven...!

Jesus, quoted in Matthew 5:11–12

Find out more

Amnesty International also have a website detailing human rights abuses around the world. Visit them at **www.amnesty.org.uk/**

The statue

At Westminster Abbey in London, there used to be some spaces on the west front, an outside wall over a main door. In 1995, it was decided to put up statues of ten Christians who have died for their faith around the world. Wang Zhiming is the last one on the right. Find out more at **www.westminster-abbey.org/tour/martyrs10-wz.htm**

What happened next?

From the late 1970s, a new Chinese government decided that attacking religion wasn't working – in fact, there were more believers in places like Yunnan than before! Instead, they tried to make peace with the Christians and paid compensation to the families of those who had been mistreated. They even rebuilt church buildings and put up a memorial stone for Wang Zhiming! At its foot may be found the words: 'They will rest from their labours, for their deeds follow them.' He is still remembered with great affection.

However, the government still allow only official 'registered' churches to exist, and the leaders of unofficial 'house' churches are still arrested and put in prison. To find out more about the current situation, visit the Voice of the Martyrs website at **www.every3minutes.com**

Juggling Balls

Thunk! Thunk! Thunk! It sounded good. He decided to throw the juggling balls at the door again, catching them as they bounced off. Thunk! Thunk! Thunk! It was like hitting a drum. This was bound to get their attention – good!

A guard came to the barred window that faced out on a courtyard and glared. 'Hey! Stop! Be quiet!'

James wasn't in the mood to stop. 'Get me a prison officer!' he replied.

A prison officer appeared, looking angry. 'Why are you doing this?'

'Because I am bored! I have been in this cell for six months, and I am still not allowed to keep all my books in the cell! You only let me have them one at a time. Why? If you don't give me the books, then I have to find other things to do. Throwing balls is fun!'

'No,' the officer replied. 'You cannot have them.'

James smiled at this. 'The prison governor said I could have them. Your government and secret police said I could have them. Do you remember?'

'They have to be checked first.'

'You've *already* seen them! I'm not talking about books that I haven't had yet. I'm talking about books that have already been in this cell!'

'They are in Rangoon.' That was hundreds of miles away.

'RANGOON? That's silly! They don't take every book I read

all the way to Rangoon!' This was getting stupid. The officer was obviously lying.

'You cannot have the books.'

James shrugged. 'Oh well, I'll just have to carry on doing this, won't I?'

Thunk! Thunk! Thunk! The sound echoed along the corridor outside his cell, then out around the prison. He had three home-made juggling balls, constructed from empty soup packets tied up with tape. James knew he was being awkward, and he knew that the guards would soon come searching for them. His whole life was now a weird game of cat-and–mouse with these people. He stopped throwing, hid one ball inside a toilet roll, and another by tying it to his leg with an elastic band. The third he kept in his hand, playing with it, throwing it up into the air and catching it again.

At noon, three guards came to his cell. As they opened the door, James decided to be polite while he sat there, playing with the third ball. 'Do you have my books?' he asked.

'No.'

'Can I write down the names of the ones I want?' He wanted a collection of poetry by Rudyard Kipling, an encyclopedia and *The Imitation of Christ*, a book about living as a Christian.

'Yes.'

'Can I keep the juggling balls?'

'Yes.'

'Are you sure?'

'Yes.' James didn't believe them, but he put the third ball down to see what they would do.

As soon as he got up to leave his cell for his daily exercise and wash, a guard snatched the third ball. So *that* was how they wanted to play it! More guards came in to search for the other juggling balls, but found nothing. James thought about the ball strapped to his leg – he would be having a wash soon! They'd see it – then what? He thought fast, then decided to take a stroll around the yard behind the cell, where they couldn't see him. Then he quickly unstrapped the ball and buried it in the earth. He could always get it later. The time to wash came. As soon as he was locked back in his cell, he found the first ball in the toilet roll and started throwing it at the door.

Thunk! Thunk! Thunk! It was a lovely noise, like a drumbeat. A guard came to the window to see what was going on.

'Will you give me my books?' James asked him.

'No!'

Oh well … Thunk! Thunk! Thunk!

Clang! The door was thrust open by the guards again. James hurled the ball out of the door, over their heads into the main prison area. At least it would give the other prisoners something to talk about. Now the guards had *two* of his juggling balls.

Later that evening, a friendly guard came to the window to give a word of advice. 'Mister James. We have been told that if you keep on making a noise, then we are to stone you.' He brandished his catapult, the sort they used to hunt the rats that were such a pest around the prison, then went away.

That made James stop and think. Would they use catapults on him? Probably – but this was getting *stupid*! The Burmese government didn't follow *any* kind of rules – that's why he was here in prison in the first place. They just thought they could do whatever they wanted, and anyone in

Bible inspirations

During his stay in prison, certain verses from the Bible became very important to James. Here are some of them:

'You shall know the truth, and the truth will set you free.' John 8:32

'If anyone has material possessions and sees his brother in need, but has no pity on him, how can the love of God be in him?' 1 John 3:17

'He has showed you, O man, what is good. And what does the Lord require of you? To act justly and to love mercy and to walk humbly with your God.' Micah 6:8

Burma who disagreed was 'an enemy of Burma'. It was a stupid argument, but they would shoot or lock up anyone who didn't agree. James had come to Burma to challenge that, and so he was thrown into prison as well – but he could still make a fuss, even over a few books. He couldn't let them win, not even over this.

What should he do now? He thought about it all night. Should he bang on the door with his fists? That was the trouble with protesting – you have to see it right through to the end. James felt afraid, and in the darkness, he decided to pray.

'Dear God, give me the courage to make this action.
Give me the strength to persist in this action.
Give me the humility not to lose my temper.
Give me the wisdom to speak sense afterwards.'

A history of modern Burma
(Union of Myanmar)

1962 A military junta seizes power in Burma. (A military junta is a group of soldiers who rule the country. Nobody votes for a junta – they just rule the country because they are the ones with the guns.)

1988 The Burmese army kills thousands of people during student protests against the military junta.

1989 Protest leader Aung San Suu Kyi is placed under house arrest.

1990 There is a real general election in Burma! Aung San Suu Kyi's democracy party (National League of Democracy) wins 80% of the vote, but is not allowed by the army to take power. She has won an election without leaving her house!

1991 Aung San Suu Kyi is awarded the Nobel Peace Prize.

1996 The Burmese Government brings in a new law that makes it illegal even to *talk* about politics in public!

He decided. Yes, he would make his protest when the prisoners were lining up on parade outside. But he would only hammer on the door for one and a half minutes. That would be enough to make his point. He remembered the friendly guard's warning: what about the catapults? The blanket on his bed *might* give him some protection, but not much.

Morning came. The prisoners were taken out from their cells and lined up in front of the guards and the Prison Governor. He held his breath, raised his fists and began.

Bang! Bang! Bang! Bang! Bang! Bang! Bang! There were angry shouts, the sound of guards hurrying over – and then they started throwing stones through the window at him! It was like being in a hailstorm! James covered his head and body with the blanket to shield himself, and carried on thumping the door until the time was up. When he stopped, the stones stopped flying as well. There was a weird silence. He stepped over to the window to see what was going on – there was quite a crowd out there, including the Prison Governor! James caught the Governor's eye and smiled.

'Don't you know it's wrong to keep someone in solitary confinement?' he called out. 'Where are my books? You won't even say *why* I can't have them!' The Governor hurried out of sight, looking quite shocked. No one normally spoke to him like this.

Then an officer ran up to the window. 'Shut up!' he shouted.

People were listening, so James kept talking. 'Why? You keep *lots* of other people locked up like this all over the country! What about Min Ko Naing, the student leader? He's not a criminal, but he's been in prison for *ten years*! You lock people up, you forbid them to speak! All around the world, it's the prisoner's right to make complaints – but not here, not here in Burma! Explain to me why I can't have the books! Give me a reason! That's all!'

The officer grabbed his catapult, loaded it and aimed it directly at James' face.

James kept talking. 'It's not me I'm complaining for – it's for everybody in this country!'

The catapult fired, the pellet whizzing past his ear.

James still kept talking. 'Give me a reason *why* I can't have the books! I'm protesting because this is all *wrong*!'

He fell silent, and the crowd started to move away. He turned to look at the inside of his cell – the floor was covered in stones, gravel and dust. He looked out of the window again. The guards were fetching stones and piling them up nearby. More of them were carrying catapults. Some were carrying large sticks as well. This was *not* looking good.

What could he do? Make some padding from his blanket and spare clothing? Hide out of sight of the window? They could still come in through the door and beat him with their sticks. How far did he want to take this? He still had one juggling ball hidden away, as if *that* mattered. He could keep thumping the door – what would happen then? Noon came. Should he thump the door again? What did God want him to do – die? Everyone has to stand up to bullies, but when can you stop?

At noon, James was let outside again for his daily exercise and wash. He thought about the ball he had buried in the yard the day before. He would have to dig it up so he could get it back into his cell and carry on with the protest about the books. It was frightening.

'God, I am so scared,' he thought as he stood there, 'but I am *not* going to give in to these bullies! I am frightened, but I am *not* going to give up until they give me the books or give me a reason why they hold them back.'

Just then, a guard came to the yard. He held three books – the Kipling, the encyclopedia, and *The Imitation of Christ*. Fantastic! He handed them all to James, who was so pleased he felt like hugging the man! He took the guard by the arm and led him round the yard to the back of the cell. Then he dug up the last juggling ball and gave it to him, as a thank-you present. The guard stared, then burst out laughing. This round of the fight was over – but there would be others.

How it all began

When James Mawdsley was 13, a Burmese boy joined his school and they became best friends. Later on, when James heard about the pro-democracy leader Aung San Suu Kyi being put under house arrest in Burma, he was filled with admiration for her and felt that he wanted to support her somehow. He dropped out of university to travel the world, and later went to Burma to live at a rebel camp in the jungle, where he taught children English.

After that, the campaigning began. In September 1997, he took a journey into the capital city of Rangoon and made a protest outside a school. For this he was deported (thrown out of the country). He did it again in April 1998, and was jailed for 99 days. Then in September 1999 he did it again, and was sentenced to 17 years in prison. He was released in the year 2000 after a lot of pressure was put on the Burmese rulers by people around the world.

Universal Declaration of Human Rights

In 1948, the United Nations General Assembly agreed on a range of human rights that would set the standard for every government to keep. It has 30 Articles (paragraphs). Here are some of them.

Article 1
All human beings are born free and equal in dignity and rights.

Article 5
No one shall be subjected to torture or to cruel, inhuman or degrading treatment or punishment.

Article 18
Everyone has the right to freedom of thought, conscience and religion.

Find out more

James now works for Christian Solidarity Worldwide, an organisation that works to defend people around the world who are persecuted for their faith. For more information, visit their website at www.csw.org.uk

James' books

James' family were able to send him books, but the prison authorities made some strange decisions about what he could or couldn't have in his cell.

He was allowed to read:
Long Walk to Freedom, the story of Nelson Mandela's 26 years in prison.
One Day in the Life of Ivan Denisovich, a story about surviving life in a prison camp.
They Have Their Exits, a true-life story about escaping from prison camps.
Dying We Live, a collection of powerful letters from people in prison for their beliefs.
God's Smuggler, about smuggling Bibles past guards.

He was *not* allowed to read:
A Diskworld novel by Terry Pratchett. (Find a booklist and guess which one!)
Mr Brave and *Mr Uppity*, two stories by Roger Hargreaves about the Mister Men!

Work that out if you can!

Sharks and Crocodiles

The sea was rough today, with a large swell that made it hard to see any great distance. Midshipman Baines was trying to use his telescope. Captain Henry Luke stood beside him on the ship's bridge.

'Baines, do you see them?' he asked.

'No, Captain … wait, yes! There she is, four miles away! A schooner … with three masts. She's large, but low in the water, heading north. A slaver, I think – and loaded. And she's flying the Portuguese flag.'

'Do you think they've seen us?'

'Not yet. She's not in a hurry. It won't be long, though.'

'Then we had better make some speed.' Captain Luke turned to the other officers. 'Gentlemen! North-north-west as fast as possible, please. Mr Kirk? Prepare a boarding party in two boats with cutlasses and carbines. Our gun crews need to be ready as well. Oh, and have the ship's surgeon in attendance.' He paused. 'To your stations, please.' They ran.

Orders were shouted, and sailors climbed the rigging to adjust the canvas sails. Then HMS *Myrmidon* turned to take the wind. She was a 20-gun sloop designed for making swift attacks on enemy shipping. As part of the British West Africa Squadron, she was on a mission – to destroy the trade in slaves between Africa and the West Indies. Suddenly, her sails filled with wind and she leapt forward to begin the chase.

Captain Luke enjoyed this type of mission. Britain had abandoned the whole filthy business of slavery, and now it was time to finish the whole thing for good. As his ship picked up speed, he felt proud.

The midshipman kept his eye on their target. 'They'll see us now. They've got to!'

Luke stayed cool. 'I'm going to fire a warning shot. Tell me if you see any slaves being thrown overboard.'

'*Would* they?' The shocked midshipman turned and stared at him.

Luke frowned. 'It's happened before. It removes the evidence. There's a lot of sharks in these waters. Open fire!' A cannon sounded with a loud bang.

'She's turning towards us! Sir, their gun ports are open! They're going to make a fight of it!'

The captain snorted. 'How very stupid of them!' He turned to another officer. 'Mr Kirk, cancel the boarding party! Prepare for battle – but remember, we *don't* want to sink them! We're here to set people free! Aim for their rigging and crew!'

There were more explosions, this time from the slave ship. 'They're trying to drive us away!' Baines shouted.

Luke grinned. 'I think we'd better show them we're not going! Open fire!' The whole sloop shook under their feet as ten cannon blasted from the port side. Clouds of thick black smoke

Fighting the slave trade

The British West Africa Squadron was established after the Anti-Slavery Act was passed in the British parliament in 1807. Several Royal Navy ships were sent on constant patrol to capture slave ships and to set free any slaves found on board. Naval officers were even offered a 'bounty' (reward) in cash for every slave set free: £60 for a man, £30 for a woman and £10 for a child! It took a long time, but the British campaign gradually made a difference over the years until the 'Atlantic trade' stopped.

drifted from the gun deck. The gunners had timed their broadside perfectly. As the port side tipped out of the water, they'd fired all their ammunition directly into the slave ship's rigging. There was a distant crashing sound as two masts collapsed. Some of their sails were burning, too.

'Prepare to turn and fire from starboard!' yelled Luke. 'This time, get the crew!'

They made another pass on the slave ship, and blasted its main deck with grapeshot. The effect was devastating and terrible. Men fell like skittles.

'They're on fire now!' muttered Luke. 'Why don't the idiots surrender?'

The flames on the slaver were spreading fast. There was a loud bang and a whoosh! of flame as some gunpowder exploded in the stern. Some of the enemy crew were letting down boats.

'Sir! Their crew are abandoning ship!'

'What about the slaves? Have they left them chained up? Good grief! Get in closer – but not too close! Mr Kirk! Send our boats over *now*!'

'Pity for poor Africans'

Before it was stopped, slavery made it possible for many British businessmen to make a lot of money from growing crops such as sugar in the West Indies. The poet William Cowper wrote this sarcastic poem about them in 1788:

Pity for Poor Africans
I own (know) I am shocked by the purchase of slaves,
And fear those who buy them and sell them are knaves;
What I hear of their hardships, their tortures and groans,
Is almost enough to drive pity from stones.
I pity them greatly, but I must be mum (silent),
For how could we do without sugar and rum?

Captain Luke watched two parties of Royal Marines row the short distance to the sinking slave ship. How many poor wretches would be chained up over there? A hundred? Two hundred? It didn't bear thinking about. Perhaps he could save some of them.

Many years later, Bishop Samuel Ajayi Crowther was writing outside his hut, at a portable desk. He was just finishing a page in his diary, when a small group of people came into view and approached the hut. They whispered amongst themselves, but then waited respectfully until he had finished – then one of them stepped forward. 'Bishop, we come from the town of Bonny. We want your help.'

Crowther was curious. He put down his pen.

'Why? I've come to this land to ask you to turn away from your old superstitions and follow the Christian God, but you have refused. You wanted to be left to do things in the old way. So, why do you now want *my* help?'

'We've heard that your Jesus can perform miracles. We want him to drive out our crocodiles.'

Crowther frowned. 'I remember your town and your

crocodiles. I saw some in the river. They're *big*, aren't they? They don't seem to be afraid of anything, either. I even saw one crawl along the street! I asked one of your people, and he said that you all worship the crocodiles. You even leave out offerings of fresh meat for them!'

The man nodded. 'That's because we're afraid of them. They are spirits of great power! If we don't worship them and feed them, then the spirits will eat our children.'

'So you worship something you're frightened of.'

The man shrugged. 'Doesn't everybody?'

Crowther looked up at the cross fixed to the wall of his hut, then shook his head. 'No.' He seemed to make up his mind about something, then rose from his seat.

'Listen, I am from the Yoruba tribe, like you. I know the way

Jaws!

The crocodiles faced by Samuel Crowther might have been 'slender-snouted crocodiles', which are native to west and central Africa, but are now probably extinct in Nigeria. (Perhaps too many were turned into steaks!) The slender-snouted crocodile prefers a fresh-water habitat, is used to a diet of crabs, shrimps, snakes and fish, and can grow to be at least 4 metres long. Give them enough of the right food and these beasties could probably grow even larger! To find out more about them (and other varieties of crocodile), visit the Crocodiles website at www.pbs.org/wgbh/nova/crocs/whos/nojs.html

things happen in these parts, but if you want God's help, you must learn to do things God's way. Does that make sense?' Some of the group nodded.

The first man spoke again. 'Some of us think the problem is getting worse. There are more crocodiles than there used to be.'

Crowther sighed to himself. Of course there are more crocodiles, he thought – you're feeding them. 'Listen,' he said. 'I want to meet your tribal elders. Tell them I have a suggestion, but they all need to hear it and they all need to agree to it, or else it won't work. We'll meet here on Sunday at first light. It *must* be this coming Sunday, do you understand?' There was more nodding, then they turned and left. Bishop Crowther watched them go. He was thinking about crocodiles – and then, all of a sudden, he was thinking about sharks. He shook his head. People can do crazy things if they don't believe in a God who loves them.

It was Sunday. The elders arrived with their chief, who sat on a special chair brought by his servants. Crowther greeted them all, then rose to his feet to speak.

'Good people, you tell me you have a problem with crocodiles. Well, I have a suggestion for you – but first, I need to tell you a story to explain it. Many years ago, I was a slave. It was on a fine morning like this when the slave-raiders came to my home town of Osogun. They burnt our house, killed my father, captured my mother and her children as well, including myself. We tried to escape, but they caught us and tied us up like wild animals. Later, I was sold in exchange for a horse – can you believe it? A horse! I was then sold on to someone else, and became so depressed that I even tried to kill myself. I had lost my family, my friends, my home and everything I ever knew. That is what slavery does to a person. It takes away everything that makes you who you are. It is as if you have died!'

His audience looked shocked. 'I have heard it was like this!' said one man.

Crowther continued. 'But I didn't die. Something made me decide to live and make the best of it. I'm glad of that now. My masters took me to the great slave market in Lagos, and sold me *again*. With hundreds of other slaves, I was put into the hold of a great ship, bigger than anything I had ever seen before. It was going to take us all away from our homeland, never to return. Can you imagine how we felt?'

'Like animals, Bishop!' said someone else.

'But then my life began to change. Our ship put out to sea, but then it was attacked. Another ship had been sent to save us! There was a sea battle, and I was taken on board this new ship. I thought the crew were going to eat me! They didn't, of course. I was being saved! I made friends with the ship's captain, was taken back to another port and sent to a school. I learned to read and write – and I also learned the greatest thing of all. Listen closely!'

The others leaned forward. Crowther was now almost whispering.

'I learned that there *is* a God who *cares* for each one of us, and this God put us in charge of the creatures of this world. He does not want any offerings, except the offering of our obedience to him. He does not feed on the blood of our children. So I could see that instead of being a helpless slave, I could *choose* to be a servant of the living God. And that is what I did. In time, I was made a minister in the Church, and that is why I am here, to talk about it to anyone who will listen.'

He paused, gazing at the listening crowd for a moment, then continued.

'But what do I see here? You are free people just as I was, and yet you have *allowed yourselves* to become slaves, just as I was! You have become slaves of a worthless religion that feeds on fear! Your crocodiles are *not* gods! They are *not* spirits! They are just animals, like the cattle you keep for food! So my suggestion to you is this. Stop being slaves! Choose to be free men again! Worship the living God who put you here to be in charge of his world, and take your town back! Be bold! Drive out those crocodiles!' He paused, then grinned. 'I hear they make excellent steaks!'

He had finished. His audience were muttering amongst themselves. Drive out the crocodiles? Could they do it? Would their people agree to it? The chief rose from his chair.

'Bishop Crowther, you have travelled to many places and seen many things. You do realise, don't you, that your suggestion is not easy? Our people have worshipped these creatures for generations.'

Crowther rose to answer. 'Yes, but where has that left you? All I see is a town of frightened people and fat crocodiles. That is the way it sometimes is with people. They prefer to keep the things they fear instead of seeking out their freedom. But you can choose to do something *new*. You could choose to be different. You could choose *life*.'

The chief thought about this, then spoke. 'Very well. I think you are right. We must take our town back from these creatures. But I am curious about something else – why did you ask us to meet you today?'

Crowther smiled. 'Because it is Easter Sunday, the day when Christians celebrate how the death of one man set many others free. He died as an offering for many, to buy their freedom.'

'Very well, Bishop Crowther. Tell us more about this freedom.' And the Bishop did.

Dedicated to who?

Ajayi was born in the little town of Osogun in 1809. Osogun was in Yorubaland, which is now part of Nigeria. 'Ajayi' means 'important'. When he was born, his parents asked a local witch doctor to find out which of the 400 traditional gods he should be 'dedicated' to, but the witch doctor warned them against it. He said this child would be *very* different!

Africans and the slave trade

In 1821, Ajayi was captured by African slave traders in a massive raid on his town. Many African chiefs made themselves wealthy by capturing and selling thousands of people from other tribes. Without their help, the Atlantic trade of African slaves could never have grown in the way it did. It's a sad fact that slavery wasn't just something that European people did to Africans. Africans did it to Africans as well. Many nations have used slavery throughout history, but the 'Atlantic Trade' still has a terrible reputation because of the sheer numbers involved (maybe 13 million people) and the dreadful way in which the slaves were treated.

Ajayi's new life

When he was set free, Ajayi was taken to the port of Freetown in Sierra Leone and sent to school. He did well, and after six months he could read and write in English well enough to teach other children as a 'pupil teacher'! (He was paid seven-and-a-half pence a month.) He also decided to become a Christian and was baptised in the year 1825. He chose a new name, 'Samuel Crowther', after the man who had set up the Freetown school in the first place.

more

Reunited!

In 1843 Ajayi became a Christian minister. (One of the guests of honour at the service was Henry Luke, the Captain of HMS *Myrmidon*.) Ajayi was very good at explaining Christianity to Africans, so he went on several 'missions' taking the Christian message to the different tribes along the River Niger. He also began work on translating the Bible into the Yoruba language. It was on one of his journeys that he discovered his mother and sisters (who were now ex-slaves) living nearby! Imagine that meeting!

Meeting Queen Victoria

Ajayi made several visits to Britain, during which time he met a lot of people including the Prime Minister and Queen Victoria. The queen was especially pleased to meet him and asked him to recite the Lord's Prayer for her in the Yoruba language. In 1864, at a special ceremony in Canterbury Cathedral, he was made Bishop of the Niger. Ajayi was the first black African to be given such a job. (Henry Luke was there as well. The Royal Navy had made him an Admiral now!) Towards the end of his life, Samuel worked on further translations of the Bible and a prayer-book into local Nigerian languages. He died in 1891.

Eternity

The Sydney bar wasn't full, but the barman was kept busy. It was hot, and the news reporters were in. They came from the newspaper office over the road, and tended to drink a lot and talk loudly, but it didn't matter. They always paid up, and were never any trouble – well, no trouble that the barman couldn't handle.

'He's mad, you know,' said one reporter. Let's call him Bert. He's middle-aged, got a bit of a belly on him, and smokes. He's seen it all.

'Who is?' asked the other reporter. Let's call her Shirley. She's young, and learning the trade of writing news stories quickly. They say she'll go far.

'That nutter who keeps scribbling those words all over the place. He should be locked up.'

'What words?'

'You mean you haven't seen them? Where've you been for the last ten years? Still at school? Don't you ever glance out of your car window when you're on the way to a story, and see it?'

'See what?' she asked.

He sighed. 'And you call yourself a reporter? Listen, you're *paid* to notice things! It's that word "Eternity" scribbled on the walls and pavements. They're all over the city, usually in chalk, always big and always in large copperplate handwriting, the sort they used to teach in schools in the good old days when children could still write! "Eternity!" He must be mad!'

Shirley looked puzzled. 'It's a funny word to write, isn't it? Kids usually scribble their own names. What's Eternity got to do with anything? Is it something political? Is it an advert for a perfume or something?'

'Perfume? Typical woman! But I haven't a clue either. It's been going on for years, and nobody's ever found out who's been doing it. There's a story waiting to be told there. Why don't you find it? Nothing much is happening, everything's quiet at the moment. It'll give you a nice piece to fill a weekend page.'

> **Copperplate**
>
> *This is printed in the style of copperplate handwriting. It's called this because it was first used for making engravings – a type of printing. The engraver would scratch the writing on a polished copper plate with a very sharp instrument and the finished writing could be used for printing copies on to paper. There are lots of curls and joins because this made it easier for the engraver, who doesn't have to keep lifting his pen so much. That's where a lot of our joined-up handwriting styles first started!*

'Thanks, but no thanks,' she snorted. 'I'm not going to become a leader writer by hunting down a mad graffiti artist.'

'All right then – let's do it together. I'm just curious, and I'm sure you *could* find an angle for a juicy story if you put your pretty little mind to it.' He winked.

'Bert! You're a fat arrogant pig, do you know that?' She smiled, and he grinned back. 'All right then,' she exclaimed. 'You're on!'

They discussed how to find the Eternity man. Bert thought it would have to be a man, of course. Women weren't that crazy. 'Let's start by being lazy. We could try writing a little piece asking who the mystery man is, and see if any of our readers know. Let someone else do the work.'

She thought about it. 'I'll write it if you answer the letters.'

'You're on.'

And so the hunt began. Their newspaper editor agreed it would be an interesting story, so Shirley wrote the piece and the editor put it in that Saturday as a nice half-page spread with a photograph. They gave it a good headline: 'Have you seen the Eternity Man?' After a week, all that came back were a few more sightings of the same graffiti, but no names. Bert read through the letters and brought them over to the bar when they had a free lunchtime.

He couldn't say very much. 'Well, whoever it is, they seem to live in Sydney. It's probably just one man, because the handwriting is always in the same style. He only uses chalk. He's probably right-handed. And sometimes he writes the same word several times along the same street.'

'And nobody ever sees him do it.'

'So he does it when it's dark. More mystery, my dear Watson!' He lit another cigarette.

'Sherlock Holmes would love a case like this, but there's no crime, is there? It's not as if writing in chalk on the road is a criminal offence. It always washes off in the next rainstorm.'

Bert sat silently for a moment, puffing smoke

up towards the ceiling. It helped him to think – at least, that's what he told his doctor, who was trying to stop him smoking. 'Perhaps we're coming at this from the wrong angle. What does the word Eternity mean?'

Shirley pursed her lips, trying to remember. 'It's … a word like … Forever … It's about something that goes on for ever and ever….'

'… Amen? Do you think this is something religious? Now, we hadn't thought of that, had we?' It was a new angle.

Shirley's next article listed all the ideas that had come in and appealed for more help from readers. Then a few days later, just before the big thunderstorm, Shirley saw him. It was about 8.30 in the morning. She was going to post some letters on the way to work, when she saw this old man, bent down on the pavement with a piece of chalk, scribbling away. With long graceful strokes, he was creating the word: *Eternity*. Who was he? She stuffed the letters in her pocket and strode over to talk to him, but he was up and off, walking down the street before she could reach him. Then she turned a corner – and he was gone. Nothing. She felt a drop of water on her cheek. Rain.

The Eternity Man – where was he? She stopped to think. Nearby, stood a church. Eternity … could he be in *there*? It was worth a try. She went to the door, pulled it open and bumped into the church minister who was coming out.

'Can I help you?' he asked.

She thought quickly. 'I'm looking for someone. An old man in an overcoat. Did he come in here?'

'An old man in an … Oh! That's Arthur!'

'Arthur?'

'He's our cleaner.' The minister called out down a corridor. 'Arthur! There's someone here to see you.' He turned back to Shirley, smiling. 'What's he done now?'

'*Now*? He's the Eternity Man, isn't he?'

The Eternity Man came down the corridor, holding a broom.

He was old and didn't look in the best of health, judging from his skin condition. One of his eyes looked a bit odd, as if it wasn't working, but he had a shy smile. The minister introduced him. 'Arthur, this lady wants to talk to you.'

Arthur looked slightly worried and spoke in a hesitant voice. 'What about?' he asked.

'Eternity,' replied Shirley. He relaxed a little.

'Now *that* would take some time,' he replied. 'Have you got a minute?'

Shirley had. She sat down, explained who she was, and with a bit of encouragement, Arthur started to talk. From outside came the rumble of thunder, and the pitter-patter of rain on the window. While he was speaking, Sydney was having its first real downpour in weeks.

'The name's Stace, Arthur Stace. Why do I do it? Well, I suppose I want people to think. You see, I used to have a really bad life. Years ago I joined the army, got wounded, came back . . . and then everything just fell apart. No family to speak of, and no home. I was drinking, drinking far too much, drinking anything – even methylated spirits. It was *that* bad, do you understand? I had nothing to live for.' She nodded in encouragement.

'Then one day, I made a decision. I'd wandered into a church service, and stayed to listen to the preacher. And *do you know*? He made *sense*!' Arthur looked around the room. 'I'd never had any time for church before. I was too busy trying to have a good time, and failing at it. That preacher said we all have a choice. We can choose either to live with God for ever, and that's called Eternity, or we can live without him. Everyone has to choose. So on that day, I chose. I made a decision. I wanted to live with God for ever.'

'You chose Eternity,' added Shirley.

Arthur nodded. 'He kept using that word, Eternity, and it was singing in my mind. It was as if that one word said everything to me. So my life changed. I stopped drinking. I found somewhere to live. I got a job here. But I wanted to share what I'd found.'

He shrugged. 'Now, I'm no talker. I can't make a speech. But I can write. So that's what I decided to do. I wanted to tell everyone that they've got a choice – to live just for the day or to live for Eternity.'

'And you've been writing that on the streets ever since – for years!'

He smiled, sadly. 'Miss, I'm a nobody, I've got nothing. But I found out that God thought I was a Somebody. So I spend my days pointing people to God.'

'Does it work?' asked Shirley.

'I don't know. But it got you into church, didn't it?' He smiled. 'Please excuse me now, miss – I've got my cleaning to

The big E

As a graffiti artist, Arthur had his problems. Somebody kept following him with another piece of chalk, altering the word Eternity to read Maternity – so Arthur started making the first E much bigger. That's how it came to look the way it did!

A changed man

Arthur was born in a slum area of Sydney in 1884. His parents were both alcoholics. As a child, he could neither read nor write and earned money by stealing. He joined the army, learned a little reading and writing, and went to fight in the First World War (1914–18). During the war he was wounded in one eye, losing its sight. His life was one long sad story until the day in 1930 when he made that visit to church. After this, everything was different for Arthur. For the next 37 years of his life he would get up at 4 am every day, pray to God to ask where he should go, and then spend hours and hours writing on the city pavements, before starting his job at 10 am.

do.' He got up, found his broom and left. Shirley wasn't sure if she had a story for the paper or not. Was anyone interested in Eternity nowadays? She thanked the minister, then stepped outside into the street again. The rain had eased off now. She glanced down at the shining pavement where Arthur had been writing. No, his message had gone, washed away in the time it took to do her interview.

She thought about her own job at the newspaper and all the things she wanted to do with her life. Did they matter? All the words she wrote for her newspaper would be read once, then thrown away. Did that have any more point to it than Arthur's words?

The sun was coming out again, breaking through the clouds. Lots of things come and go, she thought, but some things carry on. As she strolled down the glittering street, a word kept flickering at the back of her mind and wouldn't go away – *Eternity*.

The end?

Arthur died in an old people's home in 1967, aged 84. He left his body to the university for medical research, and asked that any proceeds be given to charity.

more

Arthur's last word

As the year 2000 began, the whole world celebrated the dawn of a new millennium. In Australia, someone decided to write Arthur Stace's 'Eternity' in fireworks on Sydney Harbour Bridge. It was even in the style of his handwriting. Arthur's message was now up there in lights for the whole world!

Dangerous

The end?

Margaret stood by the empty grave. She knew Janani wouldn't be buried here. The Ugandan government had sent the body to another place where there would be less fuss – and fewer questions. They didn't want him buried here. It was too close. Even when Archbishop Janani was dead, he was too dangerous for them.

The radio said he had been killed in a car crash – as if! The two main newspapers had printed pictures of the car as proof – except that each newspaper had pictured a *different* type of car. These people couldn't even tell a good lie! Margaret looked at the empty grave again and smiled sadly. The truth would keep coming back – it always did. That's the trouble with truth – it keeps bursting through like a strong wind, and the lies all get blown away in the end, like so many dead leaves.

Memories

Janani was the finest man she had ever met. Margaret had come to Uganda to work as his secretary. As she stood there, she remembered so many things. Janani could have left the country when life in Uganda became more dangerous, but he didn't. He stayed, and he hadn't kept silent. 'You *can't* keep quiet when your country is tearing itself to bits,' he'd said. He could have been a tribal chief – but instead, he chose to serve his

Janani said to a friend, 'I see the way ahead very clearly. There are storms, waves, wind and danger, but I see the road clearly.'

people as a priest, then as a bishop, and then as the Archbishop of Uganda. 'It's my job to point the way out of this mess!' he'd said. Well, *somebody* had to – Uganda was in a mess since Amin had been put in charge.

The general

General Idi Amin had come to power as President because some soldiers thought he would be a better leader than the last one. Of course, they didn't bother with holding an election. Elections were for weaklings! For them, taking power was a simple case of shooting a few guns, killing a few people and scaring everyone else so they kept quiet. That's how it happened – and Amin now ran the country as if he could do what he liked. He was like a greedy child plundering a sweet shop.

If there was any money going, Amin claimed it for himself. If there were business deals, then he had to be paid as well. Anyone who spoke out against the President was (if they were lucky) suddenly put in prison. The unlucky ones were simply taken away by soldiers and never seen alive again. People said there were a lot more crocodiles in the rivers these days. The President was 'feeding' them.

Archbishop Janani Luwum wouldn't accept it. 'Uganda is a beautiful country with good people, and it's being completely messed up! I've *got* to speak to Amin!' he said. 'He's got to be told he's *wrong*!' First of all, he met up with other Christian and Muslim leaders. They all agreed that something had to be done, so they sent a polite message to the President, asking to see him.

An angry letter came shooting back from the President. 'Who said you could have a meeting?' it demanded. 'You didn't ask my permission!' That's just the way he was.

The midnight raid

After that, things got worse. A few months later, Janani and his family were asleep at his home when, in the middle of the night, the family dog started barking – and there was a horrible crashing noise outside. Janani's wife, Mary, dashed to the window and saw that a large army truck had driven straight through their fence! Armed soldiers were jumping out and running towards the house! Janani rushed downstairs to see what was going on.

'Open up!' shouted an army officer, thumping on the door. 'We've come to search your house for weapons!' He barged through the front door as soon as Mary opened it, pressed the barrel of his gun into Janani's stomach and held it there while another man searched the Archbishop from head to foot.

'Our house is God's house!' exclaimed Janani, as other soldiers dashed in. 'We pray for the President! Why would we have guns here?' It was no use. The soldiers searched the whole house, pulling out mattresses, looking under beds and even climbing into cupboards. Of course, they found nothing because there was nothing to be found. After they had looked in every room, and even checked the chapel, they gave up. No guns here! The army officer looked slightly embarrassed. It wasn't supposed to happen like this. He went outside, then came back, looking rather awkward.

'Er ... could you please open your front gate to let us get our truck out?' he asked. 'We're stuck!'

Mary was furious. 'Why don't you go out the way you came in – through the fence?'

Janani stopped her. 'No, we are Christians. We have clean hearts and we'll show it.' With that, he went to open the gate to let the truck out. When he came back, he hugged Mary, and they went back to bed. Luckily, their children had stayed asleep through the whole raid! Everyone tidied up in the morning.

'Mum!' yelled Phoebe, their daughter, as she was looking around. 'You'll never guess what those soldiers took!'

'What?' asked Mary.

'Our bag of bananas!' said Phoebe. 'Maybe they think bananas are dangerous weapons!'

It was all so crazy and frightening, but things like this were happening every day in Uganda. The President was frightened that people were plotting to get rid of him in the same way that *he* had plotted to get rid of the *last* president. Nobody was safe now. It was like being locked in a room with a madman who holds the key to the door in one hand and a gun in the other!

The trial

Then the day came when Janani was taken away by soldiers. 'There's a special meeting for all the important leaders in Uganda,' said the officer who came in the car. 'The President expects everyone to attend!' The meeting was to be at a conference centre in Kampala, the capital city. Janani kissed Mary goodbye, and was driven to the centre with a friend, Bishop Festo Kivengere.

Lots of soldiers were waiting for them when they arrived. The two friends were quickly taken to a large open area where there were even more soldiers waiting. Nearby were some tables, laden down with a strange display of machine guns, bullets and hand grenades. As soon as the soldiers saw that Janani had arrived, they sat down. 'This isn't a meeting,' whispered Festo. 'This is a trial!'

The Vice-President of Uganda stood up and addressed the crowd.

'The President bids you welcome! We are gathered here today to hear some terrible news! Some enemies of our land have been caught plotting to kill our President and overthrow our government! Listen to their confessions!'

Some men rose to their feet. One had bruises all over his face – another could hardly stand at all. The whole group looked as if they had been badly beaten up. One by one, they were led up to a platform where, in front of the whole crowd, they were forced to explain their 'crimes'. Some could hardly talk because of their

Idi Amin – Who's laughing now?

Many people in Britain thought that President Amin was a joke and they made fun of the stupid things he said and the military uniforms he wore that were covered in medals. Amin didn't seem to mind the jokes, because it meant that he was left alone to rule Uganda as he liked. Do you think that making fun of a bully is a good or a bad idea?

Two years after Janani's death, Amin fled the country when Uganda was invaded by an army from nearby Tanzania. He first went to live in Libya, and then to a 'safe' house in Saudi Arabia, where he died in 2003. He was never put on trial for his crimes. During his years in power, approximately 300 000 people in Uganda 'disappeared'.

injuries. When they had all finished making their confessions, the Vice-President asked a question.

'So then, who was helping you?'

'Archbishop Janani Luwum!' they all replied, obviously terrified.

Festo was baffled at this stupid rubbish. What was going on? Janani turned to him and whispered. 'They are going to kill me.'

'Kill you? We've got to *do* something!'

Janani looked him straight in the eye. 'I am not afraid.' The Vice-President rose to speak again.

'You have all heard this terrible news! Our church leaders have

been plotting with our enemies!' He waved a hand towards the weapons neatly stacked in the middle. 'And can you believe it, we found all these near the Archbishop's house!' There was a gasp from the crowd. 'Nobody is above the law!' he yelled. He turned to the soldiers. 'What shall we do with these traitors?'

'Kill them!' shouted the soldiers, shaking their fists. 'Kill them now!'

'Well, let us decide now! Raise your hands, all of you who want these traitors shot in public!' All the soldiers raised their hands. 'Now raise your hands, all of you who don't want them shot.' Not a hand was raised. How surprising!

> The light shines in the darkness, and the darkness has never overpowered it.
> Gospel of St John 1:5

'No!' declared the Vice-President. 'They will be given a fair trial first!' Janani and Festo were taken to a guarded room and told to stay there while the 'trial' took place down the corridor. They would not be allowed to see the 'trial', of course. Instead, they had to sit there, listening, waiting to find out what was coming next. It was like being in a mad play where everyone else knew the script and the ending, but you didn't.

Then a guard came in. 'Everyone can go home now,' he said, 'except for the Archbishop. His Excellency the President wants to talk to him.' So Amin was here!

Janani turned to Festo and smiled. 'I can see the hand of the Lord in this.' He said goodbye, left the room and was led away. That was the last his friend ever saw of him.

Afterwards

What had happened next? Margaret had heard stories. The President had been planning to see Janani all the time – but only after trying to scare him with the false 'confessions' and 'trial'. Amin had wanted Janani to sign a 'confession' (written by someone else) in which he admitted plotting against the government. Janani had refused. So Amin's soldiers had pushed Janani to the floor, hitting him to make him sign the confession. He had still refused – so they shot him. Some said it was the President himself who fired the gun.

Janani's body had been taken away. That evening, the radio news said that he had been killed in a car crash. Next day, the government said that the Archbishop had started fighting with the driver on the way home

> One word of truth can fell a forest of lies.
> (Alexander Solzhenitsyn)

from the trial and caused the crash himself. These were just more lies to cover up the truth.

It didn't end there. His family weren't even allowed to have the funeral they wanted. A big funeral had been planned in Kampala cathedral, but the government banned it. Janani still seemed to worry them. He was dangerous even when he was dead!

The beginning

Margaret stared at the empty grave. Janani wasn't there. But wherever they'd buried the body, he wouldn't be there either. In a way, people like him didn't die. Something powerful still lived. He had died like Jesus, falsely tried and murdered. But Jesus had

A life less ordinary

Janani Luwum was born in 1922 at Mucwini, in Uganda, to a Christian family. As a boy, he spent his time herding the family's cattle, goats and sheep. He was a skilled marksman and hunter, loved climbing trees, was a dancer and musician, and as a teenager was able to walk the 80 miles to his boarding school at the beginning and end of every term. His father could not afford the school fees until Janani was aged ten, but the boy worked hard once he arrived there, and decided to become a teacher. After attending a training college, Janani worked as a primary school teacher for a few years. In 1948, at a village meeting, he made a personal decision to become a Christian, just as his parents had once done. Afterwards, he said this:

'I was overwhelmed by a sense of joy and peace. I suddenly found myself climbing a tree to tell all the others (at the meeting) to repent and turn to Jesus Christ ... I stayed up that tree for a long time!'

After that, he felt that God was calling him to be a Christian minister. He would now be teaching thousands – but not from the top of a tree!

'I love Idi Amin.'

After Janani's death, his friend Bishop Festo Kivingere was appointed Archbishop in his place. Perhaps Amin was hoping at this point that Janani's death would keep Festo from speaking out. It did the exact opposite! Some years later, Festo wrote his own book about these times, entitled *I Love Idi Amin*. He wasn't joking: like Janani, Festo said that Uganda's only hope for the future was if people learned to forgive!

beaten death and so had Janani. He hadn't bent like a blade of grass in the wind – he had stood firm against the fear. One day, when this madness was over, his country would come back to life again. She looked out over the city. Janani's death would show the whole world what this mad President was really like. In the end, that would probably save Uganda. Then the lies would be over. The truth always comes out in the end.

A story told by Janani

'There was once a middle-aged man whose wife died in childbirth, leaving him with a baby boy. He took good care of the child. He never forgot to bring him food from the garden. But one day, he decided to put the boy to the test, to find out whether he would look after him in his old age. He gave the child some potatoes as usual but on this occasion asked the boy to share them with him. The child refused and hid the potatoes from his father. Yet the old man continued to care for the boy until he grew into a man and married. Sadly, this is how we are with God. He gives us gifts and when he asks us to give him back a little of what he gave us, so that we can use it to enlarge his kingdom and help the needy, we refuse. Yet still he continues to look after us, hoping that we will change and become good children.'

The letter that sealed Janani's fate

'We are deeply disturbed ... We have buried many who have died as a result of being shot, and there are many more whose bodies have not been found, yet their disappearance is connected with ... the security forces. We know what is happening because the widows and orphans are members of our churches.'

This is part of the letter sent to Amin by Christian and Muslim leaders in February 1976. Janani personally delivered it. Some say this is what made Amin decide to have him killed.

The statue

At Westminster Abbey in London, there used to be some spaces on the west front, an outside wall over a main door. In 1995, it was decided to put up statues of ten Christians who have died for their faith around the world. Janani Luwum is there. Find out more at **www.westminster-abbey.org/tour/martyrs10-wz.htm**

Storyteller

A Melodrama for the Entertainment, Education and Improvement of Young Minds

Cast: Narrator
Hannah More, *a young lady*
Sarah, *her servant*
Sir Jasper Fowlpest, *a local farmer*
Various poor children

Setting: *A drawing room of the eighteenth century. Hannah More is sitting on a chair in one corner, telling a story to a small group of children, who are seated on the ground. She is dressed well, but they are barefoot and obviously from a poor background. Hannah is a good storyteller, and the children are listening very closely.*

Narrator: We are now going to set before you a scene that will tug at your very heartstrings! Our heroine is the fair maiden Hannah More, a brave young lady who has taken it upon herself to help the poor children of her parish, by running a Sunday School in her own house. She teaches them to read, to write, and tells them Bible stories – a most worthy cause, I am sure you will all agree! However, there are some who oppose this work – and one of them is about to try and spoil everything! When he appears, do not forget to hiss or boo, or do whatever our young child actors request! Let the entertainment begin!

Hannah: So, children, to finish our story! The wise man Daniel was thrown down into the den of lions, and the pit was covered up with a heavy lid. Thunk! Was that the end of Daniel? His enemies rubbed their hands with glee. At last this troublemaker was gone! They were so pleased. They waited for the sound of lions' teeth, to hear him being torn limb from limb!

Children: Oh no! *(A door opens.)*

Sarah: Miss Hannah, there's a man to see you. He says it's urgent! *(She looks nervous.)*

Hannah: But Sarah, I'm finishing a story! Please tell him to wait!

Sarah: But it's Sir Jasper Fowlpest, Miss, the richest farmer in our parish! He's being awfully insistent! Please…?' *(There is a thumping on the door – Sir Jasper strides in, brandishing a stick. He is obviously angry.)*

Sir Jasper: Miss More, I want a word with you!

Hannah: Sir Jasper! What's wrong?

Sir Jasper: It's this Sunday school you've started here! I don't like it!

Hannah: But why, Sir Jasper?

Sir Jasper: Because you are telling stories and teaching children how to read and write! *(Children and Sarah hold up signs saying HOORAY!)*

Hannah: But what is wrong with that?

Sir Jasper: It's wrong, Miss More – terribly wrong! It has to stop now! Send all these children away! *(Children and Sarah hold up signs saying BOO!)*

Hannah: But why, Sir Jasper?

Sir Jasper: Because these children will be my workers one day! If they start learning how to read and write, then they'll think they're as good as me. That's how revolutions start, you know, Miss More – when people lose their respect for their betters! They'll want me to treat them differently. They'll start demanding higher wages. Education does that, and education is for those who can pay for it, Miss More! *(Children and Sarah hold up signs saying BOO!)* My family had to pay out good money to put me through a decent school. And you're teaching them for free! It's not right, so it must stop today and I will stop it! *(Children and Sarah hold up signs saying BOO!)* Send these children home, or I will turn their parents out on to the streets! *(Children and Sarah hold up signs saying BOO!)*

Hannah: *(To audience)* Oh no! I must stop him! *(To Sir Jasper)* But Sir Jasper, this Sunday school is giving these children a hope and a future! Would you heartlessly tear it away from these poor little ones?

Sir Jasper: But it's not for them, don't you see? They're merely peasants! It's their place to plough and sow and reap, like it says in the Bible. It's not their place to read and write. All this learning will give them ideas above their station! They must learn to accept their place in life! *(Children and Sarah hold up signs saying BOO!)*

Hannah: *(To audience)* For the sake of these children, I must win him round or all will be lost! *(She raises her eyes as if to heaven)* Merciful God, please help me! *(To Sir Jasper)* Sir Jasper, why are you so angry? Do you really think there's harm in teaching these children their letters and telling them what the Bible says?

Sir Jasper: Yes! These children should listen to men of my class for instruction on how to work, and to clergymen in church for instruction on what to believe! They shouldn't be listening to a young woman like you! Obedience is what they need to learn!

Hannah: But Sir Jasper! Ignorance is such a terrible thing. This is the eighteenth century! Our nation should be built by people who understand, who have a purpose in life! Just suppose some of your workers could read, wouldn't that make your life a little easier?

Sir Jasper: *(To audience)* Such fine words from a mere woman! *(To Hannah)* But how, my young lady?

Hannah: Well ... *(She is thinking fast.)* You could leave written instructions for them, instead of having to explain everything. I'm sure that farming is a very complicated profession – wouldn't it be useful to have workers who knew their letters and could

count accurately? They could collect rent from your tenants!

Sir Jasper: *(To audience)* This is strange talk! *(To Hannah)* But Miss More, that's my job!

Hannah: *(She nods, as if pretending to agree with him.)* Yes – and a very busy job it must be as well, although of course I wouldn't know much about that, being a mere woman. *(To audience and Sarah)* A mere woman! I ask you! *(To Sir Jasper)* Sir Jasper, if I was in charge of a large farm with all its workers and buildings and machines, I would want to give the lesser jobs to others. It would give me more time for doing the really important things. *(To audience)* Like staying in bed on cold mornings!

Sir Jasper: *(His expression changes. There is the hint of a grin.)* Did you know, Miss More, for a young lady, you can be remarkably persuasive?

Hannah: Oh, I wouldn't know about that, Sir Jasper. It takes a man to really understand these things, don't you agree? Men are so much cleverer! *(To audience and Sarah.)* I don't think!

Sir Jasper: Miss More, I am moved by your words and your sweet manner! You have made me see this matter in a new way! I declare that the Sunday school can continue! What is more, I shall put by a sum of money for the building of a new village school, so that all the children of this parish may learn their letters and learn to count! I have seen the light! *(Children and Sarah hold up signs saying HOORAY!)*

Hannah: Heaven be praised! *(Children and Sarah hold up signs saying HOORAY!)*

Narrator: And so, ladies and gentlemen, you see how the words of a good woman can sway the heart of a hard man. The fair maiden Hannah More was able to create many Sunday schools just like this one all over the land. For a 'mere woman', she did more for the poor than many men ever did. Thank you for being such an appreciative audience – I wish you good day and farewell!

Education! Education! Education!

Hannah More (1745–1833) lived in a time when there was an incredible amount of poverty and crime in country towns and villages. How do you change things like that? She saw education as the answer. The children of the poor needed to be taught how to read and write, and to learn to love God, so that they didn't waste their lives on alcohol or crime.

Many rich people (like the imaginary Sir Jasper) thought she was completely wrong and said so in newspapers and magazines and churches. Hannah usually didn't bother to answer her critics. She just kept on setting up more schools, often using her own money to rent buildings and pay teaching staff.

The slave trade

Hannah campaigned with people like William Wilberforce and Thomas Clarkson to bring an end to the slave trade. She argued that it was stupid to say that women or Africans were less intelligent, when women and Africans weren't even allowed the same education as white European men. This did not go down well in Bristol, her home town, which was a major centre for the slave trade!

She also wrote 'The Slave Trade', a popular poem on the subject:

Shall Britain, where the soul of freedom reigns,
Forge chains for others she herself disdains (rejects)?
Forbid it, Heaven! O let the nations know
The liberty she loves she will bestow (give);
Not to herself the glorious gift confined
She spreads the blessing wide as humankind;
And scorning narrow views of time and place
Bids all be free in earth's extended space!

more

Bluestockings

As an author, Hannah knew lots of famous people in London society, but she sometimes found parties rather 'tiresome'. (That's a better word than 'boring' – try using it.) So, with some friends, she invented 'conversation parties' where you could talk about really interesting things. Her group (known as the 'Bluestockings') invited special guest speakers – like Dr Samuel Johnson, who created the first English dictionary. It was a lot more interesting than playing cards and gossiping about hairstyles! Hannah used these parties to whip up support for all sorts of campaigns, including the fight against the slave trade.

Why women can't do maths

Hannah and her sisters (Mary, Betty, Sally and Patty) were well-educated. (Hannah could read by the time she was three!) However, girls were not allowed to go to college when finishing school, because only boys did that at this time. Girls were not even allowed to learn mathematics in some places, since it was thought that such things damaged the brains of women, because they couldn't hold as much knowledge as men! Instead, the sisters set up a school for girls in Bristol and ran it themselves ...

The star!

Hannah wrote and published a great deal of poetry, drama and fiction. Most of it is now forgotten, but she was a star in her day! (She made at least £30 000 from writing, and that's worth over a million pounds now – but she gave away a great deal of it to good causes, including her schools.) She said she wanted to explain about life and God to ordinary people in ways they could understand – and in doing so, provided cheap reading matter for people who could never afford a book or a newspaper. This is one of her poems that tackled the whole problem of understanding why there is pain and suffering in the world.

Turn the Carpet

This world which clouds your soul with doubt
Is but a carpet inside out
As when we view these shreds and ends
We know not what the whole intends;
So when on earth things look but odd;
They're working out some scheme of God.
What now seems random strokes will there
In order and design appear.
Then we shall praise what we have spurned (rejected),
For then the carpet will be turned.

How to become really clever

Michael Faraday never had any science lessons. He left school early, worked as a newspaper delivery boy, and then started work in a book-binder's shop at the age of 13. Where did his genius come from?

It's simple. He read in his spare time – and discovered a book by Isaac Watts that changed his whole approach to life. Watts was a hymn writer and a thinker. His book *The Improvement of the Mind* was a brilliant common-sense guide to learning. It explained how to benefit from lectures, reading, conversation and observation, and recommended the keeping of notebooks to record interesting ideas. This made sense to Faraday, so in 1809 he began to keep one. Watts also said it was useful to attend lectures, exchange letters with other interested people, and join discussion groups. Faraday began to do all these things. Watts also said that it was important always to find out the real facts and not to be 'too hasty to erect general theories from a few particular observations'. This was perfect advice for any 'scientist', although the word wasn't invented yet– and it all started with a book...

Faraday later went to work as an assistant for Sir Humphrey Davy (ever heard of the Davy lamp?), and kept on soaking in all this learning. He was well on the way to becoming one of the finest scientists of all time – and it all started with a book.

Power Play

Setting: *A Victorian scientific laboratory, with lots of bottles and jars and interesting-looking scientific equipment on display. There is a workbench towards the back of the room, with two armchairs towards the front of the stage, half-facing the audience. The scientist Michael Faraday is wearing a laboratory apron, with his jacket sleeves rolled up. He is examining a large magnet.*

Faraday: *(talking to himself)* So, what's making this pattern? Why does the magnet concentrate its power in lines of force? It's curious. *(He holds up or points to a diagram of magnetic lines of force, so the audience can see, then he picks up the magnet.)* And … how far do the lines reach? Across the table? Outside the room? There must be a way to measure them. How? *(There is a knock at the door. He looks at his watch, impatiently.)* But it'll have to wait. *(He rolls down his sleeves and goes to the door – outside is Mr Philip Festerleys.)*

Festerleys: Mr Faraday? I made an appointment with your secretary to see you.

(He is shown in by Faraday. Festerleys is well-dressed and looks rich. He shakes hands with Faraday, sits down – and stares around the room, obviously fascinated by the strange sights and smells.

Festerleys: Mr Faraday! Thank you for making time to see me. I know you're a busy man, so I'll come straight to the point. My name's Festerleys – Philip Festerleys. I'm a businessman. I make it my business to spot new ideas and then see if there is some way they can be turned into something useful.

Faraday: *(smiling)* You mean, you see an idea and ask yourself if it can be turned into money.

Festerleys: *(smiling in return)* Well put, Mr Faraday! Yes, I like to see if there's money in it – and I'm not ashamed of that. We all wear clothes – and someone has made and sold them to us, and I see no reason why that person should not receive an honest day's wage for doing so.

Faraday: Do go on.

Festerleys: Now then, I was at your lecture last Friday evening at the Royal Institution. It was very impressive. I had no idea that such things were possible with electricity. I'm here to offer you a very interesting deal. I want to ask if you would be prepared to do some research for me, and then take a share in the profits.

Faraday: You're not the first to ask me that. Thank you, but no. I'm a scientist, not an inventor. I'm only interested in discovering and explaining the laws that govern our universe. I don't invent better mousetraps, or whatever it is you have in mind. If I discover anything that's useful, then it's there for everybody to use. I don't want to make a profit from finding things out.

Festerleys: *(looking puzzled)* But Mr Faraday, I don't think you fully take my meaning! That business of yours with the electricity – I'm not a scientific man, but I am prepared to wager that if you can discover new powers and forces, then that can be used. Perhaps … it would give us new ways of heating or lighting a house! Perhaps it would give us new ways of moving things around, better than steam power. Power, Mr Faraday! Think of it! There's always a use for power! I can tell you this – it would put bread on your table if you could let me use that power!

Faraday: I'm sorry – no. I feel a bit hungry at the moment, but there is plenty of bread on my table, as you put it, and I do not need any more.

(There is an embarrassed silence. Festerleys looks a bit puzzled. He wasn't expecting that kind of answer. However, he hasn't finished.)

Festerleys: Well then, let me talk to you about something else! Your lecture last week got me thinking. I'm still amazed at the way you constructed that remarkable wooden cage covered with wires. You sat inside it, asked somebody to throw a switch, and then all of a sudden, you were covered in electrical sparks – and afterwards climbed out, perfectly safe! It's a miracle!

Faraday: No, it's science! I was perfectly safe. That was the point! I was showing how insulators work. There was no danger.

Festerleys: But that was showmanship as well, Mr Faraday! I've heard that you always start your lectures in the same way! You just open the doors exactly on time, enter the lecture theatre quietly from the front, and then with no introduction, you start talking. It's brilliant! You can hear a pin drop when it starts!

Faraday: That's because I practise.

Festerleys: But have you ever been to a fairground, Mr Faraday? No? Well, I have. There's a man who shouts at the crowd, begging them to come in and see some sideshow where somebody throws knives or something like that – but you're doing something much more interesting! You're explaining things in a brilliant way to normal people – and they want to listen!

Now, Mr Faraday, here's my second proposition. Suppose I was to organise for you a lecture tour of the country – not in lecture theatres where only students go, but in real working theatres – and you could stage your experiments for paying customers? It would be a sensation! They'd come from miles around just to see you. You would be talking to thousands of people. Would you consider it?

Faraday: I'm sorry, but no! It would take me away from my work here. It's hard enough now, just finding the time to prepare lectures for the Royal Institution and do research as well!

Festerleys: Well then, here's another idea. Have you heard of the terrible things going on in the Crimea?

Faraday: Yes. I have read the reports in *The Times* about the work of Miss Nightingale and her nurses, and the wonderful work of Mrs Seacole too. But the soldiers must be suffering terribly.

Festerleys: Well, what if I was to suggest to you that there was a way in which you could bring that whole war to an end? It could be done quickly and cleanly. Her Majesty's Government would be very pleased. *(He taps the side of his nose, knowingly, and winks.)*

Faraday: Her Majesty's Government? I thought you were a businessman!

Festerleys: I am, but let's just say I do a lot of work for the government as well, and especially the army. Now, Mr Faraday, as I was saying, suppose there was a way of bringing that terrible war to an end? Wouldn't that be a good thing? *(He pauses for effect, then leans forward to whisper.)* Perhaps it could bring all wars to an end.

Faraday: What do you mean?

Festerleys: I'm talking about gas, Mr Faraday – gas! I know you have done a lot of research in that field. I think that we now have in our grasp a new way of fighting wars. We wouldn't need all that terrible business of riding around and shooting people! Instead, we could use gases! There might be a gas that could wipe out a whole army! Imagine that being used in the Crimea, on the battlefield, Mr Faraday! A war would be over in a day! The world would be at the feet of a man who could invent such a weapon! Just think! They'd make you a lord on the strength of it!

What did *he* discover, then?

Faraday's interest in electricity led to the discovery of electro-magnetic rotation. He found that putting a current through different materials could produce a circular movement. This was the principle behind the first electric motor. He also discovered a way to produce electricity from a magnet – and found a whole new world of magnetic fields. Then he made even more discoveries about static electricity (the sort that makes your hair stand on end), gases and light rays. Faraday's discoveries made it possible to use electricity in lots of ways.

You could become Sir Michael Faraday, Saviour of the Nation!

(There is a long silence. When Faraday speaks again, he sounds angry, but he is still polite.)

Faraday: Mr Festerleys, let me make myself clear. I am not going to be part of anything that kills other human beings. I am interested in saving lives, not taking them away. I think you would try to make money from anything – even the death of others. Mr Festerleys, I have only one thing to say to you – the Wages of Sin is Death. *(He rises from his chair.)* Our interview is over. Good morning!

Festerleys: Are you really sure? I've got another idea …

Faraday: Good morning! Excuse me, but I have to go and see someone.

Festerleys: *(as he is leaving)* But … but … you don't understand! I could give you anything you want if you'd just see things my way! *(He leaves, scowling. Faraday closes the door, shaking his head.)*

Faraday: See things your way? I wouldn't trust you to clean my shoes! *(He picks up a diary and opens it to check something.)* Now, have I got time to visit Mrs Holmes? She might still need some shopping done after having that fall. Yes. I can do it. *(He smiles sadly, shaking his head as he removes his apron. He turns to the audience.)* That's the trouble with men like Festerleys – they don't understand the things that are really important. *(He leaves the room.)*

Who owns your ideas?

A patent is a licence for an idea. If you take out a patent, it means that other people have to pay you if they want to use the idea for something else. Michael Faraday never took out a patent for any of his discoveries. This meant that others could use his ideas without paying him, but he didn't mind. As far as he was concerned, it would have been selfish to claim the credit for merely discovering what God had already made. Faraday was sometimes asked to work on developing new products for manufacturers, but he always refused. His discoveries could have made him incredibly rich, but he just wasn't interested!

WARNING!

Have you ever seen a piece of burnt toast? That could be you if you mess around with the electricity that comes from plug sockets! Never play with mains electricity! It bites back!

Science and religion

Faraday was a devout Christian who read his Bible and took its message seriously. (You can still see it on display if you visit his laboratory. His Bible looks well used!) As far as Faraday was concerned, he worshipped God on Sunday when he went to church – and he worshipped God by exploring the laws of God's universe on the other days of the week. In a reply to a letter, he wrote this:

'In my mind, religious conversation is generally in vain. I do not think it at all necessary to tie the story of the natural sciences, and religion together. That which is religious and that which is philosophical [scientific] have ever been two distinct things.'

Power-crazy!

Try these experiments at home, but ask an adult to help you! Make sure your hands are really dry – it helps.

Take a litre plastic bottle that holds fizzy drink, and empty it. (Go on, use your initiative!) Then wash it out, and leave it to dry in a warm room overnight. Then put several small pieces of paper on a table. Now, rub the plastic bottle with dry silk or woollen fabric. Then hold the bottle over the paper – or someone else's head. It'll be hair-raising. This is electro-static attraction! Experiment with other types of plastic bottle and fabrics. What happens?

Inflate two sausage-shaped balloons. Rub them with the same fabric as last time. See if you can make them stick to the wall or ceiling. Hang one balloon by a thread from something, and see what happens when you move the other balloon nearer to it. Yes – you should have electro-static repulsion as well! The balloons should react like magnets, with north and south 'poles' that attract or repel depending on which way round they go.

Find out more

Faraday's lectures at the Royal Institution became world-famous, as he explained the wonders of science in everyday language, with vivid experiments. This tradition is still carried on in the Christmas lectures for young people that happen every year. Go there one day if you can, or catch them on TV! (The Royal Institution is at 21 Albemarle Street, London W1X 4BS. Visit Faraday's original laboratory in the basement! The Royal Institution website is: www.rigb.org)

To find out more about Michael Faraday, go to the internet modern history sourcebook (www.fordham.edu/halsall/ mod/modsbook) and use their search engine to find the texts of some of Faraday's most famous lectures, especially the one about the candle! Go learn!

The book that moved the world

In 1686, Isaac Newton published his ideas in a book called *Philosophiae Naturalis Principia Mathematica* (or 'Mathematical Principles of Natural Philosophy' – that's science, to you and me!). Most people call it the *Principia*. It was very hard to understand, partly because it was very detailed and written in Latin! At the beginning, Newton declared that there were three Universal Laws of Motion:

1. Everything stays still, or keeps moving in a straight line at the same speed, unless another force makes it move or change its speed.
2. Any force acting on an object will change its motion. The amount of change depends on the object's mass and the size of the force.
3. For every action there is an equal and opposite reaction.

If you want to find out more about how these laws work, then an excellent book is *Dead Famous – Isaac Newton and his Apple* by Kjartan Poskitt (Hippo Books). These ideas completely changed the way people thought about their world. Some people even say that Isaac Newton was the first real scientist, because he believed in testing every idea to see if it worked. He made it possible to understand a great deal more about our universe. Hundreds of years later, when the first astronauts took off into space in 1969 to orbit the moon, somebody asked them who was driving. 'Isaac Newton!' they replied.

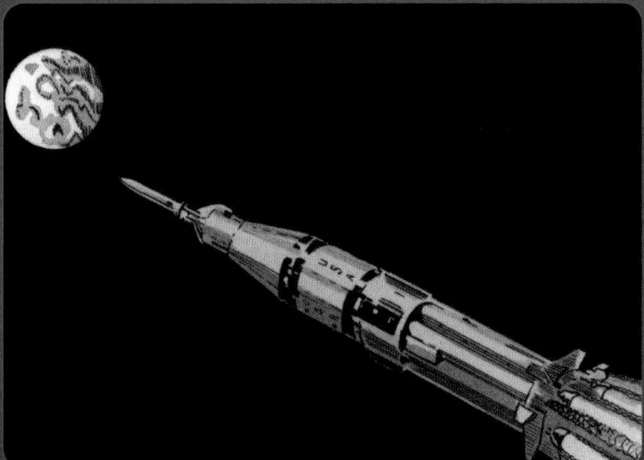

The Apple

Mr Pippin's thoughts
I hate them all, you know. They're just a bunch of nasty creatures with two legs. It's not fair! They can get up and walk around whenever they feel like it, while we trees have to stay in one place! Where's the fairness in that? It's not as if those stupid creatures do anything important. I couldn't believe it when I heard that when they eat our apples, they actually *throw away the bits with the seeds in!* It's bad enough being eaten – but it's even worse when they throw away *the most important bit!*

Mr Newton's diary
I'm not sure if it was a good idea to come home. Now I'm here, I can't settle down to anything. Why is it so hard to concentrate? Every day I sit down and try to make some notes about my work, but my mind keeps drifting. I've got to do what my old teacher said and stick to trying to solve one problem at a time, but that's so hard! Yesterday, I was day-dreaming so much, I forgot to eat my lunch!

Mr Pippin's thoughts
There he is again. He walks past here every day, talking to himself. These creatures are crazy. If I had legs, I'd be travelling around the world. What does he do? He stays in one place and doesn't go anywhere, except round and round my orchard. What a waste of good legs!

Mr Newton's diary

Why am I so different from other people? Is it a gift from God, or a curse? As a child, I remember being so fascinated by all the colours and patterns in nature that I started a sketchbook so I could draw anything interesting. Other children didn't do that. Why not? I wanted to know *why* spiders spun their webs in spirals! I wanted to know *why* snail shells are spirals! I collected dried plants and shiny stones and animal skeletons, simply because their shapes interested me. I even made little working models of machines! My bedroom became a museum and a workshop! The other children said I was strange, but I wasn't – I was just *interested.*

When I learned how to read, I discovered that books are packed with strange pieces of information and new ideas. When I found them, it was like a hungry man finding a mountain of bread. I read so much! And of course, I read the Bible, the Word of God. That *really* fascinated me! I still read part of it every day. It gives me lots of new ideas about God and his universe, but it still leaves me with *even more* questions! I'm asking questions about things that nobody has even thought about before! Is that so strange?

Mr Pippin's thoughts

He wasn't here a few months ago. He walks around the orchard every day, talking to himself, then stopping and staring at things. He even stopped and stared at *me* once, but I didn't say anything. What made him come here?

Mr Newton's diary

I miss Trinity College and I miss Cambridge. It's quiet here, so there's time to think, but I wish there were people here who could understand my ideas. The Plague's changed all that. Everyone has to keep checking their skin for the ring of horrible red spots that's a sign of infection. In the end, we were all sent home from college for our own safety – but I was so frustrated! Was that the end of my education? Luckily, I met one of my old teachers, and he put me right.

'No!' he said. 'You're a first-class mathematician! Why don't you use this time to do some research? Use the time to think, to sort out your own ideas, and write them down. If you do a good job and come up with something new, they could make you a Fellow at the college when you get back, instead of just being a student. You'd be a teacher, instead – and they'd be *paying* you to live and work there! *Think* of all the time you could spend studying *then!*'

That set me thinking. I could be *paid* to find things out? That was the best idea yet! So every day I now make notes, go for walks, talk to myself, and think. There are so many puzzles to solve – but my mind keeps wandering! It's as if I'm going round and round in circles.

Mr Pippin's thoughts

It's unbelievable! That stupid creature is going round and round in circles! When he's not walking around talking to himself, he stops to sit down right next to me! Can't he do that indoors? This is *my* orchard!

Mr Newton's diary

I'm starting to get somewhere with gravity.

I know things fall towards the ground. Everything falls down – it's common sense. Some things fall faster or slower, but that's something to do with the air in the way. I remember measuring the wind in a storm when I was a child. I jumped, and then I measured the distance it blew me along the ground. I don't think that's got anything to do with gravity, has it?

So what *is* happening out there in space? What stops the moon from falling down to the Earth, or the Earth from falling into the sun?

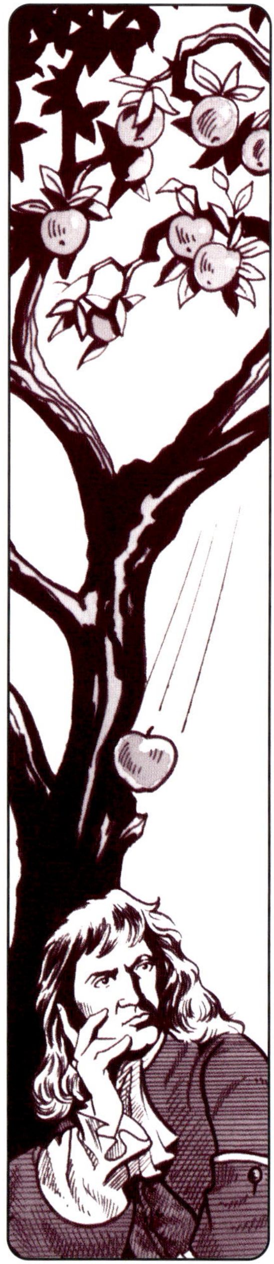

Mr Pippin's thoughts
Oh no – he's even got a little desk now. Will you *look* at that stupid creature? It's late afternoon, and he's just sitting there outside, staring at the moon! Hasn't he seen it before?

Mr Newton's diary
There's a new moon this evening, the shape of a piece of fruit when you cut a slice down to the rind. *Why* does the moon move around the Earth *at all?* I know the Earth goes round the sun, and the moon goes round the Earth in large squashed circles, but *why?*

Mr Pippin's thoughts
I've had enough of this idiot. He's been tramping around our orchard for weeks now. I'm going to get rid of him in the only way I know how! Here goes!

Thunk! Missed! Still, it made him jump! I nearly got him on the head! Now, you little twerp, will you just get the message and *go away?*

Mr Newton's diary
An apple has just landed on my desk and bounced off. Gravity again! It's everywhere! It's all part of this amazing natural order

shaped by our Creator. Things fall in straight lines, but *some* things move in *curved* lines – why? There has to be some simple explanation!

Mr Pippin's thoughts
Oh no. He's picked up my apple. He's rolling it around on his desk, catching it just before it falls off. He's mad, I tell you. He's even started to doodle in his diary, drawing big circles, with little circles inside!

Mr Newton's diary
In our universe, things start and things stop. We live and then we die. But *what* holds it all together? Is it the Creator himself? I believe in God, but I don't see an old man in the clouds holding everything in his arms like the Greek god Atlas. When I study the stars, it feels as if I'm looking inside a great clock, gazing in wonder at all the springs and wheels and weights. My God is like a great watchmaker, creating incredibly complicated patterns from the stars and planets and moons. Everything fits together and works by itself, just as it was designed to from the very beginning. But *how* does it all work?

Is the moon falling? Why does this apple fall? What's pulling at both of them?

What if … the same force that pulls the apple down was pulling at the Earth? Wouldn't the moon then crash into the Earth? But it doesn't, because … it's falling in a circle, not too close, and not too far away! Yes! The moon is always falling – *around* the Earth, because the moon is in the grip of the Earth! It's the *same* force pulling at the Moon *and* the apple *and* me!

Mr Pippin's thoughts
Oh no, look at him now! He's jumping up and down on the spot!

Mr Newton's diary
Yes! It's the same force affecting me! Big things attract smaller things! So, if I was floating out in space, would that mean that the apple would be attracted to my own body?

Mr Pippin's thoughts
Oh no! He's sat down and he's started talking to himself and writing again! *What have I done?*

How to think

Isaac didn't do very well at school. His teachers thought he was too dreamy, until one teacher saw that Isaac's lack of concentration wasn't laziness – his mind was simply buzzing about too many things at once. With the teacher's help, Isaac learned to concentrate on working at one problem at a time. Suddenly, he found that he was very good at learning from other people and finding out for himself. So the secret is – concentrate!

The 'toy' windmill

As a child, Isaac Newton made a model windmill. His friends and family thought it was just a toy, until they noticed that the sails were turning without any wind. Isaac opened up the walls of his windmill to show an intricate system of cogs, driven by a wheel. Inside the wheel were some pet mice. Every time the mice scurried forward, they turned the wheel, and that turned the cogs, which turned the sails of the windmill! When people looked closer, they saw that just like a real windmill, the wheels were also turning a miniature grindstone that was crushing wheat grains and turning them into flour, which fed the mice!

The man himself

But what did Isaac have to say about himself? Just before he died, it was this:

What did Newton believe about life, the universe and everything?

Isaac Newton would definitely have called himself a Christian, but his beliefs would have been thought rather 'dodgy', so he kept many of his thoughts to himself. Witches were still being burnt at this time, and the (very 'religious') English Civil War was still a nasty memory for a lot of people. Newton actually wrote 30 books about the Bible, more than he did about science and mathematics! However, he was also interested in alchemy (a type of magic, although he would never say that), which just goes to show that even the greatest of minds can get a bit confused. What's more, he suffered a mental breakdown in later life, probably brought on by nervous strain from writing the *Principia.*
So what did he really believe? Read some of what he had to say here, then make up your own mind.

I have a fundamental belief in the (Christian) Bible as the word of God, written by men who were inspired. I study the Bible daily.

The most beautiful system of the sun, planets, and comets, could only proceed from the counsel and dominion of an intelligent Being.

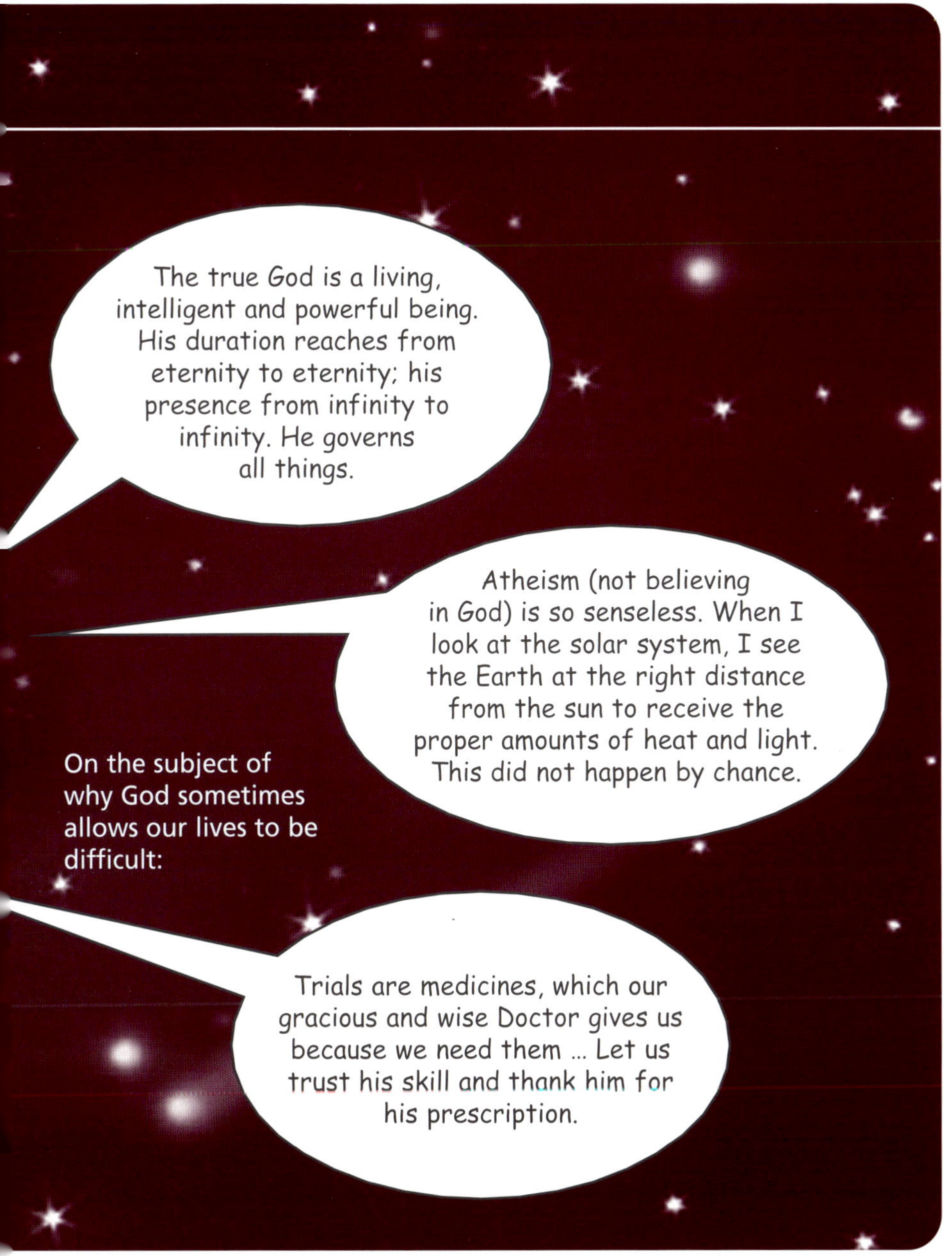
The true God is a living, intelligent and powerful being. His duration reaches from eternity to eternity; his presence from infinity to infinity. He governs all things.
Atheism (not believing in God) is so senseless. When I look at the solar system, I see the Earth at the right distance from the sun to receive the proper amounts of heat and light. This did not happen by chance.
On the subject of why God sometimes allows our lives to be difficult:
Trials are medicines, which our gracious and wise Doctor gives us because we need them … Let us trust his skill and thank him for his prescription.

Religious and Moral Education Press
A division of SCM-Canterbury Press Ltd
A wholly owned subsidiary of Hymns Ancient & Modern Ltd
St Mary's Works, St Mary's Plain
Norwich, Norfolk NR3 3BH

Copyright © 2003 Christopher K. Hudson

Christopher K. Hudson has asserted his right under the Copyright, Designs and Patents Act, 1988, to be identified as Author of this Work.

All rights reserved. No part of this publication may be reproduced, stored in a retrieval system, or transmitted, in any form or by any means, electronic, electrostatic, magnetic tape, mechanical, photocopying, recording or otherwise, without permission in writing from the publishers.

First published as *The Awkward Squad, Loud Speakers, Mind Stretchers* 2003

This edition first published 2003

ISBN 1 85175 311 7

Designed and typeset by
TOPICS – The Creative Partnership, Exeter

Illustrations by David Johnson

Printed in Great Britain by Halstan and Co. Ltd., Amersham, Buckinghamshire
for SCM-Canterbury Press Ltd, Norwich